CHECKERBOARD SOCIAL STUDIES LIBRARY

DEFENDING THE NATION

Defending the Nation

SPECIAL FORCES

John Hamilton
ABDO Publishing Company

visit us at
www.abdopublishing.com

Published by ABDO Publishing Company, 4940 Viking Drive, Edina, Minnesota 55435.
Copyright © 2007 by Abdo Consulting Group, Inc. International copyrights reserved in all
countries. No part of this book may be reproduced in any form without written permission from
the publisher. The Checkerboard Library™ is a trademark and logo of ABDO Publishing
Company.

Printed in the United States.

Cover Photos: front, Corbis; back, U.S. Air Force
Interior Photos: Corbis pp. 1, 10-11, 12-13, 16, 17, 19, 21, 27; Getty Images pp. 22, 24, 25;
    North Wind p. 9; U.S. Air Force pp. 4, 26, 29; U.S. Army p. 5; U.S. Marine Corps pp. 14,
    15; U.S. Navy p. 23

Series Coordinator: Megan M. Gunderson
Editors: Heidi M. Dahmes, Megan M. Gunderson
Art Direction & Cover Design: Neil Klinepier

Library of Congress Cataloging-in-Publication Data

Hamilton, John, 1959-
  Special Forces / John Hamilton.
    p. cm. -- (Defending the nation)
  Includes index.
  ISBN-13: 978-1-59679-759-8
  ISBN-10: 1-59679-759-2
  1. Special forces (Military science)--United States--Juvenile literature. 2. United States--Armed
Forces--Commando troops--Juvenile literature. I. Title II. Series: Hamilton, John, 1959- .
Defending the nation.

  UA34.S64H355 2006
  356'.160973--dc22
                                                                        2005032870

Contents

Special Forces... 4

Timeline 6

Fun Facts 7

History of the Special Forces... 8

Training.. 12

Special Forces Weapons... 14

Army Rangers.. 16

Green Berets 18

Delta Force.. 20

Navy SEALs.. 22

Marine Corps Force Reconnaissance.............................. 24

Air Force Special Operations.. 26

Future of the Special Forces... 28

Glossary 30

Web Sites.. 31

Index... 32

Special Forces

The United States has one of the most powerful militaries in the world. The army, the navy, the air force, and the Marine Corps use their regular fighting forces to defeat America's enemies. However, some missions require **stealth** and surprise instead of open combat. For these sensitive assignments, each military branch trains and equips **elite** groups of special operations forces.

The USSOCOM emblem

Special operations forces, or commandos, are trained to perform secret attacks. Commandos tend to work in small groups. They travel deep into enemy territory to destroy transportation routes and weapons. They are also trained to capture or kill important enemy leaders. Special forces missions are often **classified**.

The United States Special Operations Command (USSOCOM) oversees special operations forces. Created in 1987, it coordinates missions for Army Rangers, Green Berets, Delta Force, Navy SEALs, and Air Force Special Operations Command. And since 2006,

Commander of USSOCOM, General Bryan D. Brown, pins a military service award on a soldier.

USSOCOM also oversees highly skilled troops from the Marine Corps.

Today, special operations forces are often used to combat international **terrorism**. These troops help preserve the peace and security of the United States. The soldiers of today's U.S. special forces are volunteers. They freely give their time, and sometimes their lives, to defend their country.

Timeline

1676 - Special forces were used for the first time in American history.

1776 - Colonel Thomas Knowlton led a group of rangers during the Revolutionary War.

1942 - The Army Rangers were founded.

1962 - The Navy SEALs were formed.

1977 - Colonel Charles Beckwith formed Delta Force.

1987 - The United States Special Operations Command (USSOCOM) was created.

1990 - The Air Force Special Operations Command was formed.

2006 - USSOCOM began overseeing U.S. Marine Corps Special Operations Forces.

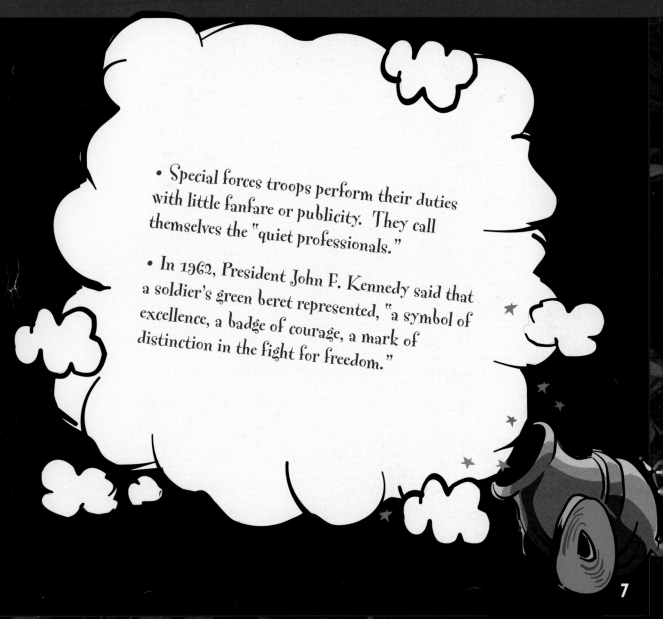

- Special forces troops perform their duties with little fanfare or publicity. They call themselves the "quiet professionals."

- In 1962, President John F. Kennedy said that a soldier's green beret represented, "a symbol of excellence, a badge of courage, a mark of distinction in the fight for freedom."

History of the Special Forces

Special operations forces have long been used by the world's armies. Rulers from ancient Roman emperors to U.S. presidents have used special forces troops. Leaders value these soldiers for their ability to **undermine** enemy forces and their use of **stealth** and surprise.

The earliest use of special forces in American history was around 1676. During **King Philip's War**, colonial forces used skilled woodsmen as scouts. These scouts were able to prepare troops for what lay ahead. Then, the troops used stealth to sneak up on the enemy.

Nearly 100 years later, Captain Robert Rogers commanded special forces during the **French and Indian War**. Beginning in 1756, he employed frontiersmen from the forests of Massachusetts and New Hampshire. They were skilled at sneaking up on their foes. They also tracked enemy troop movements.

Beginning in 1776, Colonel Thomas Knowlton led a group of rangers during the **Revolutionary War**. Brigadier General Daniel Morgan also led rangers during this war. These special forces were trained for scouting missions. They also conducted raids, or surprise attacks, and gathered information about enemy forces.

Also during the **Revolutionary War**, Colonel Francis Marion from South Carolina led a group of special forces called irregulars. They **disrupted** the British forces by using **guerrilla warfare**. And, Marion and his men hid in swamps to avoid capture. This fighting style earned Marion the nickname "Swamp Fox."

Francis Marion National Forest in South Carolina is named for the Revolutionary War hero.

The United States also used special forces during the American **Civil War**. Southern Confederate and Northern Union troops each used groups of rangers to capture enemy supplies. They also wrecked railroad tracks and captured enemy locomotives.

The United States officially formed the Army Rangers in 1942, during **World War II**. They were modeled after British

commandos. The Army Rangers used small groups of highly trained soldiers to raid and **disrupt** the German and Japanese militaries.

From 1945 to 1991, the United States and the Soviet Union were enemies in the **Cold War**. During the war, the two countries did not fight directly. Instead, they each took sides in conflicts in smaller countries. The use of special forces troops became very important in some of these conflicts. This was especially true during the **Vietnam War**.

Special forces troops were some of the first American soldiers sent to Vietnam. There, they performed **sabotage** missions. And, they helped train Vietnamese Special Forces teams. Today, the United States increasingly relies on its special operations forces. These forces are vital in the war against **terrorism**. Where **stealth** and secrecy are required, special forces will continue to carry out important missions.

A group of Army Rangers called Merrill's Marauders fought in Burma during World War II. These soldiers were specially trained in jungle warfare.

Training

Special forces training is long and difficult. Each branch of the military has its own type of special operations troops. These groups each have different training requirements. But, they are all very demanding.

Few soldiers even qualify to begin special forces training. All special forces troops must be physically fit. Still, training is so difficult that injuries are common. Only the strongest soldiers, both physically and mentally, will finish.

Commandos tend to work in small groups, so they must be experts in a variety of skills. Candidates receive combat and weapons training. Special forces troops must also be skilled at navigation, first aid, and parachuting. Candidates train day and night to become part of **elite** special forces teams.

Every part of special forces training prepares these elite soldiers for future missions. Their mental strength is tested as they are pushed to their physical limits!

13

Special Forces Weapons

Special forces troops are equipped with a variety of firearms, explosives, and other equipment. Every special forces group uses

M4A1 rifle

the M4A1 (CAR-15) rifle. The M4A1 is lightweight and can have a shotgun attached to it. If needed, this rifle can be fitted with night vision equipment and grenade launchers.

The M9 Beretta is the preferred pistol of the special forces. It is reliable, light, and easy to hide. Special forces troops also use sniper rifles to fight enemies from long distances. These firearms include the M24 and Haskins .50-caliber sniper rifles. A sniper using a Haskins rifle can hit a target more than half a mile (.8 km) away with a single shot.

For more firepower, many special forces teams use Heckler and Koch MP5 submachine guns. Even more powerful machine guns include the M249 5.56-mm Squad Automatic Weapon and the M24G 7.62-mm Light Machine Gun. Both of these weapons can be mounted on a vehicle. But the M24G usually takes two soldiers to operate!

Special forces use many kinds of explosives. C-4 is powerful and can be molded like clay. Special forces also use hand grenades that are filled with an explosive. To stun an enemy, they use flash grenades. These are especially effective when rescuing **hostages**.

Night vision goggles help special forces troops see even on the darkest evenings. This can be a tremendous advantage against an enemy.

The M24 Sniper Weapons System is strong, lightweight, and vital to many missions.

Army Rangers

The Army Rangers are the U.S. Army's **elite**, highly movable troops. They can attack from land, sea, and air. Formed in 1942, today's Army Rangers are used for many missions. They receive assignments that cannot be completed by regular army forces. And, they sometimes help other special operations groups, such as Delta Force commandos.

Ranger training is fierce. Soldiers learn to parachute from airplanes. They alight from helicopters on special ropes, climb mountains, and carry heavy battle gear. Rangers are trained to face a variety of combat situations with little food or sleep.

Due to their training, Army Rangers can be sent all over the world. They can operate in harsh places such as jungles, mountains, or deserts. Common ranger missions include quick raids, attacks, and secret information-gathering trips. These elite soldiers strike rapidly to capture enemy airfields and other targets.

Each medal or decoration on an Army Ranger's uniform represents the accomplishments of the soldier or the soldier's unit.

Army Rangers are ready for
whatever challenges they may face.

Green Berets

Some Army Rangers who are especially talented train to become Green Berets. Green Beret troops go on secret missions deep inside enemy countries. These missions often involve surprise attacks or information gathering.

Green Beret troops are required to know a foreign language. This is because they often work with groups from other countries. Green Berets help these people fight governments that are enemies of the United States.

Green Berets usually work in groups of 12. These groups are sometimes called A-Teams or Operational Detachment Alpha (ODA) teams. ODA teams can work secretly for weeks inside enemy territory without help from regular army troops.

One especially important Green Beret mission is to secretly "paint" enemy targets with lasers. Then, "smart" bombs and missiles can guide themselves to the laser-painted targets. Bombing is much more precise when forces use laser-guided weapons.

Green Berets is a nickname of the U.S. Army Special Forces. It comes from the color of the berets the soldiers wear, which are the official headgear of their uniform.

Delta Force

Delta Force is another special operations team within the U.S. Army. It is the most **elite** of all the army special operations groups. Colonel Charles "Chargin' Charlie" Beckwith formed Delta Force in 1977. President Jimmy Carter authorized its organization to combat the rise in international **terrorism**.

Delta Force is so secret that the army doesn't officially admit that it exists. So, its training methods are closely guarded secrets. Members are selected from various parts of the U.S. Army, depending on their special skills. Delta Force commandos remain among the best-trained people in the U.S. military.

Today, the main job of Delta Force soldiers is to respond to terrorist threats. They go on missions deep in enemy territory to prevent terrorism. Their missions might include gathering intelligence, or information, or capturing known terrorists. Delta Force members are also specially trained to rescue **hostages**.

Delta Force soldiers train with helicopters. So, they may be put into or taken out of dangerous situations as quickly as possible.

Navy SEALs

The SEALs are the U.S. Navy's **elite** special operations force. SEAL stands for Sea, Air, and Land. Today's Navy SEALs were officially formed in 1962. However, their origins go back to **World War II**. At that time, sailors who were expert swimmers were used for underwater demolitions missions. These missions involved swimming underwater with explosives to destroy enemy targets.

Navy SEAL training is very difficult and takes more than a year to complete. SEALs receive advanced weapons and combat training. In addition, they learn to use many types of underwater vehicles and breathing devices.

This Navy SEAL's medals and badges include the Purple Heart. This badge is awarded to soldiers wounded or killed in action.

Due to specialized training, Navy SEALs are particularly skilled at underwater missions. In addition, they are capable of attacking targets on land. They also gather information to help regular ground troops. Navy SEALs can fight an enemy in the Arctic, the desert, the jungle, or the city.

Navy SEALs perform some of the most dangerous missions of all

SEAL Delivery Vehicles allow SEALs to launch from a submarine and travel underwater.

special operations forces. Their missions often include fighting **terrorism**. And, they are still sent to **sabotage** enemy targets. SEALs also train and supply groups of foreign fighters that are friendly to the United States. And, they are specially trained in **hostage** rescue.

Marine Corps Force Reconnaissance

The U.S. Marine Corps insists that no single marine is more **elite** than another. As far as this branch is concerned, all marines are considered special operations troops. In fact, marine special operations troops rotate back into the regular marine service after just three to five years. In this way, the marines hope to show that they consider the whole branch to be special forces. But since

Marines practice rescuing hostages from sea and by air.

2006, U.S. Marine Corps Special Operations Forces have been included in USSOCOM.

Marine Expeditionary Units (Special Operations Capable), or MEU(SOC)s, are stationed worldwide. In this way, they can respond to any conflict in a timely manner. Supporting MEU(SOC)s are Marine Corps Force **Reconnaissance** (FORECON) units. These special teams perform dangerous tasks.

Today, FORECON units are trained to rescue **hostages** and conduct secret raids on enemies. They secretly gather information about an enemy. Often, FORECON missions include amphibious action. This means they work from ship to shore.

Air Force Special Operations

The U.S. Air Force **elite** special forces unit was formed in 1990. It is called the Air Force Special Operations Command (AFSOC). Sometimes, AFSOC troops work together with other special operations groups. These include the Army Rangers and the Navy SEALs. Together, they carry out search-and-rescue missions for people injured or lost on the ground. AFSOC forces can also provide cover fire for ground troops. This is called close air support. It involves shooting at an enemy from airplanes or helicopters while ground forces also attack. For this, AFSOC often uses its fearsome AC-130 gunship.

Some members of AFSOC are commandos who fight on the ground. They can arrive by land, sea, or air. This includes parachuting deep into enemy territory. These commandos fight in highly trained groups called Special Tactics Squadrons (STS). STS teams can capture enemy troops or even entire airfields.

The AC-130 gunship is nearly 40 feet (12 m) tall, with a wingspan of nearly 133 feet (41 m).

Future of the Special Forces

The U.S. military plans a bigger role for special operations teams in future conflicts. Regional wars require small groups of soldiers that can fight using speed and **stealth**. This fighting style is also important in the current war against **terrorism**. Special operations forces are ideal for this job.

Within the military, special operations troops are considered second to none. So, continued emphasis on excellence among special operations forces will be very important.

In the future, technology on the battlefield will become more advanced. Progress in technology will continue to give U.S. troops an advantage on the battlefield. Intelligent, highly trained special operations soldiers will be able to fight using the newest weapons and equipment available. This guarantees that U.S. special operations forces will be ready for whatever the future holds.

New aircraft, such as the AFSOC's CV-22 Osprey, help special forces complete missions more effectively. The Osprey can change between a helicopter and an airplane. So, it can carry out missions on its own that would usually require more than one type of aircraft.

Glossary

civil war - a war between groups in the same country. The United States of America and the Confederate States of America fought a civil war from 1861 to 1865.

classified - kept from the public in order to protect national security.

Cold War - a period of tension and hostility between the United States and its allies and the Soviet Union and its allies after World War II.

disrupt - to throw into disorder.

elite (ih-LEET) - of or relating to the best part of a class.

French and Indian War - from 1754 to 1763. A series of battles fought for control of land in North America. England and its colonies fought against France, its colonies, and several Native American tribes.

guerrilla warfare (guh-RIH-luh) - warfare that uses unusual small-scale methods, such as sabotage and raids, to weaken an enemy.

hostage - a person held captive by another person or group in order to make a deal with authorities.

King Philip's War - from 1675 to 1676. A war fought in New England between British settlers and Native Americans. This war led to further westward expansion.

reconnaissance (rih-KAH-nuh-zuhnts) - an inspection the military uses to gain information about enemy territory.

Revolutionary War - from 1775 to 1783. A war for independence between Great Britain and its North American colonies. The colonists won and created the United States of America.

sabotage (SA-buh-tahzh) - to damage or destroy something on purpose. Sabotage is often carried out by a person who wants to harm an enemy nation.

stealth - an action or a behavior performed in a secretive or sneaky manner.

terrorism - the use of terror, violence, or threats to frighten people into action. A person who commits an act of terrorism is called a terrorist.

undermine - to weaken secretly.

Vietnam War - from 1957 to 1975. A long, failed attempt by the United States to stop North Vietnam from taking over South Vietnam.

World War II - from 1939 to 1945, fought in Europe, Asia, and Africa. Great Britain, France, the United States, the Soviet Union, and their allies were on one side. Germany, Italy, Japan, and their allies were on the other side.

Web Sites

To learn more about the U.S. Special Forces, visit ABDO Publishing Company on the World Wide Web at **www.abdopublishing.com**. Web sites about the U.S. Special Forces are featured on our Book Links page. These links are routinely monitored and updated to provide the most current information available.

Index

A

Air Force Special
Operations Command
4, 26, 27
aircraft 26
American Civil War 10
Army Rangers 4, 10, 11,
16, 18, 26

B

Beckwith, Colonel Charles
20

C

Carter, President Jimmy
20
Cold War 11

D

Delta Force 4, 16, 20

E

enemies 4, 5, 8, 9, 10, 11,
14, 15, 16, 18, 20, 22,
23, 25, 26, 27, 28

F

French and Indian War 8

G

Green Berets 4, 18

H

helicopters 16, 26
hostage rescue 15, 20, 23,
25

K

King Philip's War 8
Knowlton, Colonel
Thomas 8

M

Marine Corps Force
Reconnaissance 25
Marine Expeditionary
Units (Special
Operations Capable)
25
Marion, Colonel Francis 9
Morgan, Brigadier General
Daniel 8

N

Navy SEALs 4, 22, 23, 26

R

Revolutionary War 8, 9
Rogers, Captain Robert 8

S

sabotage 11, 23
Special Tactics Squadrons
27

U

U.S. Air Force 4, 26
U.S. Army 4, 16, 18, 20
U.S. Marine Corps 4, 5,
24, 25
U.S. Navy 4, 22
United States Special
Operations Command
4, 5, 25

V

Vietnam War 11

W

weapons 12, 14, 15, 18,
22, 28
World War II 10, 11, 22